Prayers for the World

Ray Simpson

All that moves on the earth
bless your God;
all that swims in the water
bless your God;
all that flies in the air
give glory to God who nurtures us all.

Parents and children
bless your God;
friends and lovers
bless your God;
musicians and sports folk
give glory to God who nurtures us all.

Parks and play areas
bless your God;
streets and shops
bless your God;
homes and gardens
give glory to God who nurtures us all.

Creator Spirit,
may air and elements praise you,
may flowers and fabrics praise you,
may floor and desktop praise you.

Your people praise you at the dawn of the day;
may birds and buses praise you,
may work and heat praise you,
may grass and growth praise you.

Your people praise you in the midst of the day;
may eating and talking praise you,
may thoughts and actions praise you,
may male and female praise you.

Your people praise you at the end of the day;
may night and day praise you,
may the seven days of the week praise you,
may all the good that has been done praise you.

We give you thanks
because earth's life and fruitfulness flow from you,
and all times and seasons reflect your laws.
We give you thanks
because you created the world in love;
you redeemed the world through love;
you maintain the world by your love.
Help us to give our love to you.

On your world, Lord,
your love descend today.

On all who work, Lord,
your love descend today.

Where there is strife, Lord,
your love descend today.

Where there is neglect, Lord,
your love descend today.

On your world, Lord,
your love descend today.

Our Father in heaven,
your kingdom come,
your will be done,
on earth, as in heaven.

In our pleasures,
your kingdom come;
in our leaders,
your kingdom come;
in our gatherings,
your kingdom come;
on the roads,
your kingdom come;
on the networks,
your kingdom come;
in each thing we do this day,
your kingdom come.

Make whole the leisure and activity of this day;
restrain its hostile impulses,
fill its moments.

God of the call, we give thanks for the saints
and pray for those who feel thwarted in their vocation.
May they do on earth as the saints do in heaven.

God from whom all truth and justice flow,
we pray for the rule of law to prevail.
May we do on earth as the saints do in heaven.

God of resurrection, in their worship
may our churches bring honor to you;
joy to the people, and healing to the land.
May they do on earth as the saints do in heaven.

Where people long for an end to injustice,
    shine into their hearts.

Where people long for conflict to cease,
    shine into their hearts.

Where people long to right inhumane working conditions,
    shine into their hearts.

Where people long to restore the scarred places of earth,
    shine into their hearts.

Where people long for dignity in human relationships,
    shine into their hearts.

The earth is becoming a wasteland:
Breath of the Most High, come and renew it.

Humanity is becoming a battleground:
Child of Peace, come and unite it.

Society is becoming a playground:
Key of Destiny, open doors to our true path.

The world is becoming a no-man's land:
God-with-us, come and make your home here.

Among the hungry,
among the homeless,
among the friendless,
come to make things new.

Among the powerful,
among the spoiled,
among the crooked,
come to make things new.

In halls of fame,
in corridors of power,
in forgotten places,
come to make things new.

With piercing eyes,
with tender touch,
with cleansing love,
come to make things new.

Desire of every nation, we bring to you
those who are empty and who long
to find meaning.
Come to them, Lord Jesus.

Desire of every nation, we bring to you
those who are overlooked and who long
to know their worth.
Come to them, Lord Jesus.

Desire of every nation, we bring to you
those who are exploring, but who do not
know what they search for.
Come to them, Lord Jesus.

Wisdom, permeating creation and informing all peoples,
come and bring us the mind of God.

Shaper of peoples, who through Moses gave guidance
that would make a people great,
guide us into the ways of true greatness.

Bedrock, Sign of community,
come to places of instability and root them in realities
that nothing can destroy.

Key to Destiny, unlock our potential and our capacity to
serve others,
that we may be mentors and soul-friends amid
a needy people.

Light-Bringer, illumine places of darkness, despair,
and disease.

True Fulfiller of Desire, harness our deepest longings to
your infinite purpose of love.

God-with-us—the Presence that cannot be taken
from us—may we live with you and you live in us.

May our homes be gladdened by the love of parents,
the laughter of children, the wisdom of elders,
the memory of ancestors;
no word or thought to darken the day,
no memory or hurt to ruin the night,
songs and stories to open the doors of joy.

As we look into the face of the babe of Bethlehem, the face of defenceless love, in your mercy look upon your troubled world. Fear and violence, homelessness and pollution, grief and anxiety stalk it.

Move the hearts of governments and peoples to use your gifts of wealth and skill to build your kingdom of love, where we shall live free from cruelty, neglect, and fear, free to look into the face of every person with welcome.

You are among us, Lord, as you were in the homeless babe in the stable.
As we come face to face with eternal goodness, may the human spirit be renewed.

Echoes a prayer of George Appleton

Lord, may each of our lands find their peace and their destiny in your will.
Give us the dynamic that calls out and combines the moral and spiritual responsibility of individuals for their immediate sphere of action.
We pray for an uprising of people who give leadership free from the bondage of fear, sorry for the blindness of the past, soaring above ambition, flexible to the direction of your Spirit, reaching out with generous hearts to neighboring peoples.

High King of heaven and earth
from whom all authority flows,
may the diverse authorities of our times
acknowledge you as the Source of Life,
emulate you as the Servant King,
and fear you as the Judge of Truth.

May Christ set this land free
from the bitterness of memories,
and the power of the past to control the present:
the victory of the Cross over neglect and fear,
the victory of the Cross over hatred, and division.

God bless the countries of the world. Make us, your family, mindful of one another, good stewards of your earth, a blessing to the world.

Give us wise leaders, clear vision, and an understanding of what is right.

Inspire in us true values, so that the wealth and work of each land may be available to all and for the exploitation of none.

May we be a sign to the world of unity in diversity.

May we work toward a prejudice-free, hate-free, fear-free world.

May our mission be each according to their ability, to each according to their needs.

In our lands, may employers, employees, and shareholders work together like fingers on a hand stretched out for the common good.

In our leisure, may we learn to celebrate with joy, to let a thousand flowers bloom, and to delight in one another's creativity.

May we know ourselves, know what is good, and know when to stop.

May our foreign policies be to earn the trust and gratitude of our neighbors.

Give us such a sense of responsibility that,
shunning false pride and narrow interests,
we may honor one another, seek the common good,
and live as fellow citizens of your eternal kingdom.

May our nations be freed from the bondage of fear, rise above
selfish ambition, and become flexible to your direction.

May the qualities that make democracy function flourish:
homespun qualities of faithfulness, honesty, and care.

Help us never to forget that the blessings of prosperity and
peace come from eternal vigilance in the struggle against greed,
neglect, and injustice.

Free us from the resentment, mistrust, and pride
that divide and confuse our peoples.

Give us a heart to serve the poorest peoples of the world
through fair trade and friendly dealings, and yet to cherish our
own minorities who feel threatened by change.

Kindle in us a sense of purpose and a knowledge, so that each
can make a difference when we are linked to the Source of all.

Transfigure this earth,
may flowers bloom on it;
transfigure this earth,
may peace reign on it;
transfigure this earth,
may faith grow on it;
transfigure this earth,
may friendship thrive on it.

Transfigure this earth,
may people and animals be friends on it;
transfigure this earth,
may the scarred places be healed on it;
transfigure this earth,
may our bodies be resurrected on it.

Bring to birth a community of justice:
we pray for the powerful
who impose their will on the weak—
may they come to know your defenseless love;
we pray for those who seek revenge
through acts of terror—
may they come to know your defenseless love;
we pray for those who have lost limbs or loved ones—
may they come to know your defenseless love.

Lord God Almighty, wean the people from the false gods
of fortune, fame, and fantasy.
Teach our world that we have to reap what we sow.
Raise up children to serve you as the living God.
Teach us, in the spirit of Elijah, to go to you in glory.

Have mercy on little ones abused—
may tender angels draw them to your presence.
Have mercy on those in trial—
may healing angels lift them into your presence.
Have mercy on souls at death's door—
may holy angels escort them to your presence.
Have mercy on we who remain—
may smiling angels radiate to us your presence.

May the love of the Three
give birth to a new community.
May the yielding of the Three
give birth to a new humanity.
May the life of the Three
give birth to a new creativity.
May the togetherness of the Three
give birth to a new unity.
May the glory of the Three
give birth to a new society.

Guardian of the children, we pray for young people who
falter and stumble through life;
come to them in your mercy,
help them to grow in stature and to walk well with you.

As love-bearers drew out the songs the cowherd
dared not sing,
bring to flower in your people the seeds that dormant lie.

We pray for those who have none to encourage them;
bring the seeds of confidence in them to flower.

We pray for those who are trapped by
their circumstances;
bring the seeds of freedom in them to flower.

We pray for those who find it difficult to learn;
bring the seeds of understanding in them to flower.

We pray for those in the margins of society;
bring the seeds of empowerment in them to flower.

We pray for those who lack food or friendship;
bring the seeds of abundant life in them to flower.

We pray for those who are weak or nearing
the end of their earthly journey;
bring the seeds of praise in them to flower.

Help us to sense your presence among us, O Christ:

> in the gentle touch,
> in the listening ear,
> in the patient toil,
> in the concern for the poor,
> in the challenging of wrong.

Mary's Son, my friend, come and bless our kitchens,
> may we have fullness through you.
Mary's Son, my friend, come and bless the soil,
> may we have fullness through you.
Mary's Son, my friend, come and bless our work,
> may we have fullness through you.

May every lone parent and child
be cherished as Mary cherished Jesus.

May each person who seeks a place to sleep
not have the door shut in their face.

May those who work on the land
be as aware of your presence as were the shepherds
near Jesus's birthplace.

May those who are out in the cold
find a welcome as warm as the stable.

Child of Humanity—
Trinity's only Son,
gentle and strong—
from whose line we were born,
bring your peace to your warring children;
peace between rich and poor;
peace between believers and unbelievers;
peace between parents and children.

Caring Father, in you we live and move
and have our being.
Sustain those who excavate the minerals,
create textiles, grow crops, or rear cattle;
give us wisdom to manage technology
for the world's good;
bless all work done today that enables the human
family to be clothed, fed, and housed in dignity, receive
a fair return for their work,
and celebrate the gift of life.

Great Spirit, whose breath is felt in the soft breeze,
we seek your strength.
May we, and the peoples of the world,
work in dignity and walk in the beauty of the day.

Into your hands, O God, we place our families,
our neighbors, our brothers and sisters in Christ,
and all whom we have met today.
Enfold them in your will.

Into your hands, O God, we place all who are
victims of prejudice, oppression, or neglect;
the frail, the unwanted.
May everyone be cherished from conception to the grave.

Into your hands, O God, we place all who are
restless, sick, or victims of the powers of evil.
Keep guard over them.

Ground of all being, all peoples come from you.
May we honor one another and seek the common good.

Reconciler of all people, employers, employees, and
shareholders who are like fingers on your hand,
may the wealth and work of the world be available to all and
for the exploitation of none.

Unity of the world, from you all peace, all justice flow.
May we cherish the web of life and respect the rule of law.

Jesus, who lost everything,
we bring to you those who have suffered loss of work,
mobility, and well-being.

Jesus, defenseless victim,
we bring to you those who are victims of violence,
abuse, and false accusation.

Jesus, alone and destitute,
we bring to you those who are lonely,
homeless, and hungry.

Great God who mothers us all,
gather the sufferings of all
into the communion of the crucified Christ.
Shield and deliver us,
and look on each one with your merciful gaze.

O God, you called all life into being.
Your presence is around us now,
your Spirit enlivens all who work.

Impart to us wisdom to understand your ways,
to manage well the tasks of this day.

Make us co-creators with you,
so that when day fades we may come to you without
shame.

We pray for this world you have given us,
for the planting of seeds
and for the propagation of stock
in the soils and commerce of the world.

Encircle those who can neither sow nor reap
because human ills have drained them.
Give us wisdom to manage technology
for the world's good.
Sustain those who excavate the minerals,
create textures, grow crops, or rear cattle.

God of community,
Spirit of energy and change,
pour on us without reserve or distinction,
so that we may have strength
to plant your justice on earth.

Your kingdom come, your will be done on earth,
as it is in heaven, in the people and places we name.

May our nation find your will as her destiny,
and God-guided representatives at home and abroad.
May she find peace within herself and become
a peacemaker in the international family.

PRAYERS FOR THE WORLD

Copyright © 2005 Ray Simpson
Original edition published in English under the title
PRAYERS FOR THE WORLD by Kevin Mayhew
Ltd, Buxhall, England.
This edition copyright © Fortress Press 2019

All rights reserved. Except for brief quotations in critical articles or reviews, no part of this book may be reproduced in any manner without prior written permission from the publisher. Email copyright@augsburgfortress.org or write to Permissions, Fortress Press, PO Box 1209, Minneapolis, MN 55440-1209.

Cover image: Cover photo by Stockphoto24 from iStock
Cover design: Emily Wyland

Print ISBN: 978-1-5064-5950-9

www.ingramcontent.com/pod-product-compliance
Lightning Source LLC
Chambersburg PA
CBHW052038070526
44584CB00020B/3154